Piano in the Dark

SEAGULL
BOOKS
•
CELEBRATING
40 YEARS

NANCY NAOMI CARLSON

Piano in the Dark

LONDON NEW YORK CALCUTTA

Seagull Books, 2023

Text © Nancy Naomi Carlson, 2023

ISBN   978 1 8030 9 170 9

British Library Cataloguing-in-Publication Data
A catalogue record for this book is available from the British Library

Typeset by Seagull Books, Calcutta, India
Printed and bound by WordsWorth India, New Delhi, India

for my mother

CONTENTS

I

The Last Word • 3

Translating the Body • 4

An Excess of Dreaming • 5

The Half-Life of Memory • 7

Coming To • 9

Sequelae • 11

Calder's Menagerie • 13

Lockdown Aubade on Rimsky-Korsakov's Birthday • 15

"Everything in nature contains its violence . . ." • 16

Vigilance • 17

Painted Moon • 19

How Skies Fall • 20

Inward-Looking • 21

Feast of Tabernacles • 23

Small Griefs • 25

After I Swallowed the Willow Tree • 27

Translating the Dead • 29

II

Three Years Post-Chemo • 33

Mannequin Head • 34

Quarantine: Day 40 • 36

Tintoretto Blues • 37

Day 166 • 38

Viva the Vagus • 40

Aubade • 41

On the Fourth Platonic Virtue • 42

Out of an Absence of Caution • 44

After I Xeroxed the Sky • 46

My Goyishe Ex-Husband • 47

"If soil can resurrect daffodils . . ." • 49

Forever-Bound • 50

Good Sense • 51

Decreation • 53

This Life We Follow • 55

Why Sturgeon Leap • 57

III

By Any Other Name • 61

Ode for Three Exes • 63

Still-Life in Orange • 64

Ant Hills • 66

In Defense of Polyamory • 67

Bookends • 68

Etiology • 70

Trisomy • 72

Dog Star • 73

In Other Words • 75

We Weren't So Jewish Then • 76

Odalisque • 77

Sequoia • 79

Nocturne • 80

Corpse Flower • 82

Variations on a Samuel Beckett Riff • 83

Finding / Keeping the Beat • 84

Acknowledgments • 87

I

THE LAST WORD

The world's last word travels mouth-to-

mouth as in prayer or a plague

through grasslands, pampas, tundras,

fields of ice, sliding through time.

It has parted the painted lips

of emperors, lapped enslaved lips.

The orphaned word breaches the gate

of sound, cratering distant moons.

The betrothed have made of it an offering.

Newborns have lost their lives in its arms.

The world's last word strews the canal's

path with dust of fallen leaves. It forgets

its name. It forgets that it had a name.

It has no word for this forgetting.

Our organs sing in different keys
like sirens in a sea of blood.
The body feels before it knows.

Easier to read disease in leaves
drooping from unseen root-rot or mold.
The body feels. Before it knows

rain's coming, it's sensed in the bones
or in vessels flooding the head.
Our organs sing in different keys:

major for liver and lungs;
minor for tonsils and thymus gland.
The body feels before it knows

the language of dormant cells
awakening, spreading like jimsonweed.
Our organs sing in different keys,

shipwrecked in growing storms—
defiant and desperate for places to hide.
Our organs sing in different keys
the body feels before it knows.

AN EXCESS OF DREAMING

It takes an effort to summon
the sacred bird of invention—
go slowly, with caution

as Montaigne warned
against getting mired in the liminal
space between the visible and the not,

citing two cases as proof:
Gallus Vibius, gone mad
from obsessing on madness

and the convict pardoned
on the scaffold, struck dead
by his own wild imaginings—

and some nights I've let that bird
preen her feathers at my pillow's edge,
leaving several in her wake.

I've tried to wean myself
from an excess of dreaming,
but my good intentions equal

what Aquinas might have called sloth,
bothered more by too much
sleep than drink,

and Einstein might have praised,
as things restrained return in force.
Late to rise, I'm also late for bed,

maybe waylaid by a waxing moon
or a word or phrase shooting past
white space like a star.

.

THE HALF-LIFE OF MEMORY

How stable are memories—
the kind you most want to forget,
as if forgetting could bring back

the whole of the life that was
before, before that year when you lost
a good chunk of your breast

and your hair fell out in clumps,
down to each forsaken follicle—
that year you held your breath

as rads infested your body like fleas
and your blood counts fell so low
you had to loop a surgical mask

behind your ears just to breathe—
that same year your father
kept asking the date, the year,

as he curled into his pain on a
hospice pad, strains of Grieg
played and replayed by the aide

who dosed his morphine death.
How quickly a body disintegrates,
unlike this memory, its half-life more

than the cobalt lodged in my tumor bed—
even more than Carbon-14—
ten thousand years, its slow decay.

COMING TO

My mother's swoons began

with a racing pulse and her lips

turned blue. My daughter folds

into herself. When pain

or the thought of pain hijacks

blood from my brain, I reel

toward the swelter and dust

of the ground, faintly aware

of sheep bells muting

the growing gap between worlds.

As the body short-circuits itself,

loosens its grip but lingers, all reflex

and nerve, how far is too far

down this slope

tangling time and place?

Still, you persist in rehearsing

dying, though here and there

something catches your eye—

pleasure fluorescing in shades

of blues and greens flecked

with gold—a sunlit pond

as seen from below

the water's surface, and you

with your legs trapped

in lily stems, hearing the current

lap at the sides of your capsized boat

with a swoosh . . . swoosh . . . weak

as your warden heart

or what your conscious mind

might let slip.

SEQUELAE

The six hours of my first infusion—
vein in the crook of my right arm
still good, still willing to let in the medley

of caustic chemicals hung from an IV stand—
was not the real fear, nor the bald woman
beside me, turned suddenly stoplight-red,

in the throes of cytoxan gone rogue
on this, her fourteenth round,
nor the fact that they ended her treatment

and said they could do no more.
Nor the next three months when I cycled
through twitches in eyes,

blisters in mouth, full-body hives,
fever, and panic attacks—
not to mention the blood counts that sunk

like dead weights after each round,
and though white cells and platelets
would right themselves, those red cells

kept losing ground. The real fear
was not the need for a PICC line
threaded up to my heart, with the threat

of a thrombus clogging the vena cava, nor
blood that crowned the edge of gauze
and might cause me to bleed out.

Not even the days spent in bed, propped
against the wall, too tired to read,
nor the nights, despite fatigue,

when no amount of tea with mint, or lavender
spray or even Xanax could knock out
the real fear: the resolute pulse of the clock.

Duchamp called them *mobiles*—
early crank-driven works
of kinetic art, perhaps descended
from prehistoric peepal leaves
amusing an infant strapped
to a bent-backed mother

gathering berries and grains,
or the *tintinnabulum* of ancient Rome
that belled wanton-eyed deities—
not yet evolved into symphonies
of parts balanced by fragile wires,
charged by your touch or breath.

Lyrical inventions, Sartre said
of his friend's later creations—
flowers that die when motion stops—
like Paleolithic vines frozen
and locked into their S-shapes in open-
mouthed Ice Age caves

or this high-wire act on homespun
thread outside your window, suspended
like Calder's *Spider*, black disk
and cantilevered legs playing dead
until you *tap tap* on the pane,
and it twitches once like a blink,

before turning back into sculpture
the way tomorrow's quarantine days
morph into months already passed—
reminding you to throw open the sash,
let in the new autumn air, let it play
your heart like an aeolian harp.

LOCKDOWN AUBADE
ON RIMSKY-KORSAKOV'S BIRTHDAY

This violin solo teases the spring air, undulates
like a veil and shimmies to a high

"G"—the leitmotif for Scheherazade conjuring
concubines, sailors, and rocs to save her life

from her sultan husband who's sure
all women ring false and flighty.

To secure their undying affection, he orders
the death of each of his virgin brides,

beheaded the morning after the wedding vows.
Accompanied by harp arpeggios for one thousand

and one nights, the blue Sultana weaves chords
into tales within tales, whirlpools within seas, and now

on our first of untold quarantined dawns,
may we be sustained by a handful of plucked strings.

~

for Roxanne Miller (2.9.1949 – 11.1.2020)

Everything in nature contains its violence:
honeybees trading lives for stings;
electromagnetic waves beheaded for violets.

The human voice can shatter a glass of wine
thanks to sound waves and resonant frequencies.
Everything in nature contains its violence:

hydrangea globes laced with cyanide;
fresh-killed catgut strings for violins;
wavelengths of yellow and green rejected by violets,

those ancient flowers of mourning. Like Whitman's "I"
they contradict themselves, contain multitudes.
Does everything in nature contain its violence,

like a teratoma you always had? The kind
—with hair, teeth, muscle, bone—that grows?
Nothing to stop the malignant wave spreading like violets,

coming back wild each spring, rhizomes finding
their way underground, roots shooting out of nodes
to form wave after wave of invading violets.
Not everything in nature contains its violence.

VIGILANCE

Like immortals, they're reborn
each year, despite the cutting back.
My backyard hydrangeas hog the azalea's light,
beautiful and deadly when swallowed

with a compound that morphs into cyanide,
though dried and smoked
they yield a cheaper-than-pot high.
My scientist father never shared

that trip with me, sticking to complacencies
of soil and pH: acidic to yield true blue
and alkaline for pink.
Were he still alive, I'd have confessed

how I mistook a magnified view
of Covid-19 for hydrangea,
with their clustered cells,
like the mutinous clutch taken

from my breast right after he died.
After months of kill-cure in my veins,
then rads burning through the tumor bed—
six years of screenings and self-exams,

looking for that thing you so don't want
to find—my annual mammogram

pilgrimage came due.
Early pandemic I'd put off the visit, cobwebs

collecting beneath the side-view mirrors of my car,
but July brought a flattened curve
and a lull in Maryland deaths led me to don
a mask from my chemo stash and hold my breath,

as images bloomed on the digital screen,
cloudy as Saharan dust, now on its northerly trek,
swirling its plume to feather our sunsets
with shades of scattered light.

Tonight in Provence, Saint-Rémy,

the moon rises, juicy and fat—

the one van Gogh impaled

on a cliff, near stacks

of wheat-crusted gold. The cliff

still stands, though pine trees

obscure what he saw a century

of summers ago. Focus on these:

blue and not-blue cliff, orange-yellow

moon, shimmering-grain sky—

and know they survived an artist's

descent into a starless night,

though cliff and sky turned dark

at times, even black, and moon

waned cold and pale.

Tonight she sings what she knows:

how like a heart the earth expands

to hold what it must;

how deaf to our call is the ringer of bells.

Is it any wonder no one took heed,
as the god of greed pulled that wooden horse
through the city gates, the insides bristling
with Achaean spears, not unlike
how our bodies harbor
flaws in the code, pulled out
into our waking, pre-programmed
telomeres eroding to slow nubs,
dogged as Telemachus
hot on his father's trail?

Fated to be right and not believed,
Cassandra warned the Trojans
to look the gift horse in the entrails,
she, the Chicken Little immemorial,
foreseeing the fall of Troy
and even her own demise.

Too much riddle to unpack,
too much doom to swallow,
the bodies' early warning system
fails us as it failed the ancients, no match
for what we refuse to see until double vision
and buckling legs bring us to our knees,
and even then we implore time
to right our self-indulgent cells.

INWARD-LOOKING

Benign, yet still you endure
a few stitches behind your ear
to not be hoodwinked
again, though no piece of cake
to flush out what lies beneath flesh,
leaching you from you so slowly
you might not wise up
until systems go haywire.

So you keep an eye on
whatever you can,
though occluded by hope
you won't find what you try
to unearth, submitting
to sound waves bounced off organs,
electromagnetic fields slicing
your core.

You check in with your macula
with annual visits to retina mavens
who ping lights that blind your rods and cones,
mapping whether that nevus is versed
in the doctrine of manifest destiny.

Back home you use the Amsler grid
to see if any of four hundred squares

have gone wavy or blurred or are misaligned,
even as Lady Doom vogues
behind each of these doors.

FEAST OF TABERNACLES

Through the windswept din
in her head, my mother hears
Piaf's *La Vie en Rose*,
Indira Gandhi's chitchat
sharing photos of grandchildren,
the Concorde's next-to-last rattle,
but never Hebrew blessings,
not having learned to pray,
to keep kosher or take meals
in a tabernacle—temporary shelters
fragile as flesh—housing
our memories, fragile as faith itself.

My mother is caught in a sandstorm
swirl, eyes burning—
why are those bodies sprawled
across the desert?—calls for help
as dreams overtake her waking
and waking overtakes her dreams.
Gone the names for days and months,
but not my voice on the phone
as I call her to turn to the trees
and their yellowing leaves,
small tabs on this season
when my neighbors carouse

in huts strung makeshift with gourds
to remind them of sukkahs
our ancestors pitched to keep
the Sinai sun at bay.

Lost in the sands of her wandering
my mother's soles burn
in the wilderness
now that fever has gripped her body,
forced her from her own bed
with purple-and-crimson yarn
to lockdown—white curtains limp
against white walls, dawns
skipping by like lambs.

SMALL GRIEFS

In the woods on the other side
of your chain-link fence where does
and fawns paw at the frozen dusk
and a lone fox slinks across a clearing
on the prowl for something small,
even so, these bedsheets
won't stay buried: the satin ones clotted
with blood from the eight-week life
your cervix would not hold; the teal ones
draping your chest where they cut the lump
from your breast—

              your own cells, like termites,
boring through hidden ducts, bound to gorge
on your blood and gnaw at your bones;
the layette ones—so pale against bluing skin—
wound tight around your newborn son
when they ferried him from the birthing room
to machines that purred breath,
until his lungs rejected even this purified air.

So many sheets—

              even the worn-out wedding ones—
layered like the silent snow that beds
the tracks of the deer, the fox, and your own
clumsy footprints, that cannot hide
the body's betrayals piling up faster each year,

though you sacrifice parts of yourself
to keep the peace, but the body
always wants more—imperfect coffer.

AFTER I SWALLOWED A WILLOW TREE

After I swallowed the willow tree,

I began to sprout

twinned stems from ring fingers,

baskets from hollowed ears.

A hive of bees

crowned me queen.

They promised to bring me spoils

of flight, but I demurred.

From my hands sprung a meadow

that led to a stream.

I stooped for a drink,

draining the river dry,

revealing a penny wedged

between two reeds.

Heads or tails, I bet the lark.

She called tails as we watched

the coin arc past our eyes,

then plunge headfirst into my palm.

Her lament caused me to weep.

I swallowed her song, and through me

the earth ceased to mourn.

TRANSLATING THE DEAD

You never felt as close
to the newly shoveled earth as when,
echoed thud on wood still fresh
as the rending of ribbon pinned
over the heart, she left you
directives, like a trail of stones,
to guide the shiva.

But the days that follow fall
like smoke when the yahrzeit flame
dimmed, and January snow annulled
each hour of passing,
so all days revert to that Monday,
stuck in time like her last words
bottlenecked, mouth gaping
for one more breath.

It was enough to see her lips move,
like a silent-movie actress heard
through the piano's frantic flourishes,
cheeks shaping the air into gasps,
each breath made more palpable
than the last.
                    You replay the reel
of her life when gardenias bloomed
in her laughter, her lips an open book,
your own life unconceived.

With your own fingers you brush
her brushstrokes, listen before you sleep
and wake with nothing to keep
from drowning in this alien language.

Even the weather is foreign—wind
that expresses hungers hollowed—
need a knot in each gust revived.

II

THREE YEARS POST-CHEMO

My husband built a six-foot-long chain-link fence
to thwart the deer, though some called it
overkill. He saved our hosta, tomatoes

and heart-shaped leaves of potato vines
needled with holes, their runners groping
the tango of tubers below.

Also spared, the summer squash,
their throbbing yellow blooms exuding
maleness in midsummer heat, while the ladies

preferred the cooler days of mist and rain,
making the mornings when both showed up
rare as the days I could bear again

to be touched. I'd daub my finger in pollen
with a tenderness I'd reserved for my scalp,
after the last of my hair had fallen out,

then rub the inner folds of each female bloom—
even the one with a droning presence inside.
Room enough for both in this garden plot:

bee in ecstasy, and me on bent knee,
skin to soil, trusting this bee with such faith
in nectar, venom sac anchored in air.

MANNEQUIN HEAD

After my hair fell in clumps down the drain

a week or two after my first infusion

as I'd been warned but hadn't believed,

I repeated a mantra I'd heard: "Better saved

than gone to grave with eyebrows intact."

I shaved what was left, though too late to donate

to Locks of Love or fashion a wig,

or even accent a cap concealing what I'd lost.

I hid under hoodies and hats,

since I hadn't the knack for twisting scarves

into elegant knots that would stay in place.

I pinned the sheitel I bought

from a Reisterstown shop to a Styrofoam head.

By then, every hair on my body had fled,

down to the very last lash. I rouged my cheeks,

drew on some brows and plumped and colored my lips.

Strangers would tell me they liked my "style."

I felt obliged to repeat my medical tale,

like a thirty-second ad on endless loop.

They'd bring up friends who'd been cured,

as if sharing a surplus of luck.

My hair began to fill in—buzz-cut straight, at first,

then curls, thicker and tighter than ever before.

Somewhere past the two-year mark, a new do:

no explaining, you just say "thanks."

QUARANTINE: DAY 40

> We find it hard to believe in plagues that crash down
> on our heads from a blue sky.
>
> —Albert Camus

When the winds began to move
through the elms like a giant
communal sigh, I mistook the sound
for rain—the kind that washes clean
any contagion on doorknobs and decks
or the flagstones lining the garden path—
but in the flood light's reach,
just ruffle and flux of branches and leaves,
and trunks veering away from plumb.

A diversion from forty days of wandering
room to deserted room in a scene
from *La Peste*: "Rats died in the street.
People died in their homes.
The newspaper's chief concern was the street."

Lightning laced the sky,
unleashing a salvo of pea-sized hail.
By morning the robins' singsong patter resumed,
despite dead-tree limbs strewn over grass—
some impaled like stakes.
One sheared-off branch dangled
high above my head, like a sword dancer
caught in a tangle of tree.

TINTORETTO BLUES

Backed up to the county divide, this line of traffic

sputters for miles then stops, then starts again,

like a soulful tune scratched through the heart.

Twin bridges loom, suspended from Tintoretto-blue,

cloudless, smooth as the skin on a new lover's back.

How to trust the promise of parapet and truss,

cables strung to hold more than they can bear?

Oh, better to become the wind

and wield the sun like an artist's brush

defines shape and surface, droplet and wave—

then become the wave, pulled and pulled again,

embracing the weight of each body's crossing.

Didn't we just start wearing
our summer whites,
surrendering to the warming
season, and now our labors
bring us fall—
sundresses marooned
in the backs of our closets,
shadowed by gray
like these shut-in
months of plague where each day
dissolves into the one before?
Have we outgrown the rules
for what's taboo to wear
after a certain tilt of the earth
toward the sun, when shadows
lengthen like hemlines?
Something has changed
or is slipping away,
or maybe we're the ones
who've changed, no longer bound
to the altar of good intentions—
our *thou-shalt-nots*—
what we don and doff at will,
having learned our rules
no longer seem to matter,
like the missing words of a niggun.

Gone are the givens—talismans
we clung to, believing
we might be spared in some way
by marking our doors
with our own sacrificial blood.

I fall for you every time I look
at blood, especially when my own
gurgles into a test tube or drib-drabs
onto the floor, or when my knees
lock from standing too long
in one place, or even when I eye
a needle pointed at me. Once

you refused to intervene
when a migraine sucked me into
its funneled vision—so deep
I had to retreat to Holy Cross
where Sister Demerol led me
down verdant pastures
dotted with blooms as purple
as Elvis's '56 Cadillac. You,

longest of nerves sprung
from gray matter, tendril
south, dominatrix of diaphragm
walls, where you respond to every
deep belly breath I release
like a voodoo Sin City doll
with a slow leak. *Rest and digest*,
soothed as fright gives up the fight,
takes flight, and I croon,
retuning my vagal tone.

AUBADE

Another quarantine morning hovers
over your bed to overtake the dark.
There must be fifty ways to leave these covers.

Sweep back the blackout curtains that shutter
your eyes, take a swipe at your alarm.
Another quarantine morning hovers,

spreads like birdsong, the clean scent of clover.
Nothing can stop the sun's diurnal arc—
not even the fifty ways to leave these covers.

Your legs feel like peanut butter.
You can't gather strength in your arms.
Another quarantine morning hovers.

No need to dress, don't stress or over-
think, and devote the day to your art—
there must be fifty ways. To leave these covers,

stop thinking of bodies that won't be recovered.
Make a wish on the morning star.
Another quarantine morning hovers.
There must be a way to leave these covers.

OF THE FOURTH PLATONIC VIRTUE

Not a question of restraint
but, rather, of temperance,
that Major Arcana tarot card—
androgynous persona performing
a balancing act: one foot in water
and one on land,
and wings to split the difference.

Montaigne preferred to walk
on level ground, focused on solitude,
the feel of his soles on the earth
in his pink-blossomed orchard.
"Archers who overshoot marks
miss as much as when falling
short," he mused, equally
squinting from looking up
toward the midday sun
as looking down into a dark abyss.
Not "overfond" of the apples
his trees would come to bear,
he favored the melons he'd sown—
but only by the slightest of margins.

Let's face it, we're drawn to excess:
sweets and pills, whiskey and moods
like those of my bipolar ex

who couldn't live without the highs,
until they laid him low.
                    Anything good
can be taken too far, like too deep
a sleep that drags us down that slope
toward forever, or scrubbing our stains
too hard or rubbing our bodies raw.
Even too much knowledge can weigh
on us—the culture ID'd
in a petri dish; the X-ray's shadowy truths,
and like a boy with an apple perched
on his head, we close our eyes, hoping
the arrow will cleave the juicy heart.

My too-soon-dead ex and I honeymooned
in a rented cottage on Sanibel Island.
We walked the beach one afternoon,

keeping track of the pink-scalloped roof
that would guide us back to our boardwalk.
As the night chilled and the sky turned

dark except for a new crescent moon,
we retraced our steps, but all the hotels
lining the beach looked the same,

their exterior lighting dimmed
to preserve the scenic view.
We should have counted our steps,

or timed how far we'd progressed—
just as a decade later, Peter should have
tracked the flutters in his chest

before drowning in his own blood—
but I was under the spell of the shells,
and adjusting my breath to the slow

burn of a sunset, though cracks
in the firmament could be felt even then,
as we left the shore to wander the maze

of streets and jacaranda trees,
hungry and tired, but riding a wave
I thought would never let us down.

AFTER I XEROXED THE SKY

After I xeroxed the sky, I gave copies

to those enclosed by the dark.

The crew of a Russian submarine

asked for dozens if they could be spared.

One went to Henny, bedridden for weeks,

waiting for broken bones to fuse.

The widow down the street asked for three—

to cover each mirror's dazed reflection.

The dying kept begging for more.

The copies seemed less than perfect

to my discerning eye—sun a cat's eye

shade of canary, rather than gold,

and what was to be the pure blue

of heaven seemed a withered shade.

Most would not guess that white-out

was used for clouds. Only the purists—

those sweet suicides—could tell.

MY GOYISHE EX-HUSBAND

For eighteen years he was the chosen
one to knead the challah dough:
yeast and sugar dissolved in a tepid bath,
oil mixed with eggs, flour sifted on top.
Flour dusted his hands like pollen,

like ash— what we might have buried
if given the chance, before our baby,
born blue but alive, was whisked away
and we, not knowing to question
Jewish law—"Halacha"—our son deemed

"stillborn" for not having lived out a month.
A mishap of DNA was to blame,
though what were the odds
that our bloods—mine Ashkenazic, and his
from a Swedish coast—would carry

the same mutant gene?
We couldn't keep grief from our home
or from sticking to skin,
unlike the dough whose lumps we tried to best—
a pinch of flour one at a time—

so it could rise, more than itself,
to be rolled into ropes of three or six,
then braided like hair of the Sabbath Queen

and left to rise again on a parchment tray,
before baked to a perfect gold.

~

If soil can resurrect daffodils,
each spring or my mother's hosta
chewed down to level ground,

and if a stand of aspen
can share genes and a life force
so when one tree falls

its rhizomatic roots create
new clones, like the ones in Utah
over eighty thousand years old,

and if garlic bulbs can germinate
from a single garlic clove,
and spuds from sprouting eyes,

then if we could dig the deepest hole
to deposit the shrouded bodies we love—
past moonstruck rock,

past granite, past gneiss
layered like eons of grief,
past the molten rock core teeming

with elements salvaged from dying stars,
then ascend to antipodal points—
could we find their resurfaced selves?

FOREVER-BOUND

You offer a braid of hair or a breast
to the goddess of second chances who doles out

luck like confetti pirouetting in air
from her many sets of bracelet-clasped arms.

You trade tremors and thinning bones
and numbing in your soles

to reduce the recurrence risk.
Your fear seems forever-bound,

fueling your heart to race for cover
or filling your veins with lead

or worse—a dread that makes you pass out—
leaving it to chance to break the fall.

No time to consider butterfly effects,
adverse or antipodal, intended or un-

or a bit of both, like monsoons or love
or your worst fear shrouded in layers

of terror itself, or even death—
by water, fire, air or earth—elementary luck

in what grounds you in the end.

GOOD SENSE

Like Ethiopian wolves,
I turn nocturnal with need
to translate the dark, silences
filled with loving voice mails
left by the recent dead
who promise to call me back.

Had I the good sense to pattern
my days by the chariot of the sun,
I'd write paeans at dawn, but
I prefer to make my hay by moonlight
while you sleep, sweet dreamer,
the closest I've come
to a sound choice in mates.

And like Rachmaninoff's "Vocalise,"
sung with its one orphaned vowel,
I'm in a C-sharp minor mood tonight,
restless for barred owl shrieks
through the cracked-open window
of late fall—something to dissipate
fears that gather like flies to a wound,
not the least of which are reports
that my night owl ways
may syncopate my body's
circadian rhythms, may even
abridge my life.

My internal clock measures two minds:
one steady as a metronome,
rocking in time to my mother's
calibrated tones; the other
like a mare racing to the warmth
of the barn for the night
beats a path back to bed.

DECREATION

> For we are wrong side upward. We are born thus. To re-establish
> order is to undo the creature in us.
>
> —Simone Weil

I am awash in ambient noise: the air
clearing white in an even hum,
the long low sighs of my aging dog,
the keyboard tapping beneath my fingertips.

The more the room reserves from me, the more I hear.
If I unplug the air cleaner and shut my eyes,
it might be the blood moving through my veins,
my lungs with their fill and filter in repose,

or even the muffled chambers of my heart
keeping subterranean time.
In anechoic chambers, you become
the only instrument of your worldly sounds.

My second ex-husband insists we can neither
know real silence, nor the absence of light.
In the darkroom where he processed film,
his eyes would dilate so wide that the ceiling

begat constellations of stars—tiny pinpricks
of sun too weak to penetrate, unlike those flashes
that scared me one night—vitreous pulling
on retina—after a surgeon lasered my eye.

Bright as the Northern lights,
they appeared unbidden in my vision,
bypassing the optic chiasm.
Less dramatic, the craquelure on the lens

replaced after years of wear—
like a hairline crack in a marital cosmos
that grows into a slow decreation
that can't be restored by glaze or God.

THIS LIFE WE FOLLOW

What if we created a god
to give ourselves a history
to pass down to the next

in line—*l'dor v'dor*—
to be known as "the chosen,"
engraving in stone the laws

that annulled all the other
gods before—the calf
from molten gold, the ones

carousing on Mount Olympus
or buried in the bowels
of the underworld?

What if this life we follow
turns out to be a maze of dreams
no divine ball of thread

can untangle, and we can't
remember the hedge
we just left in the shadows—

like my father, sacrificed
to the Minotaur,
his mind slowly devoured?

What if the terrorist cells
hidden in some remote
strand of our chromosomes

refuse to bow down before
anything we can think of to thank
when the fever finally breaks,

the aura dissipates,
the blocked blood
finds a detour home?

WHY STURGEON LEAP

Could leaping be hardwired into sturgeon
brains since the late Cretaceous,
for no other reason than feeling good,

the way cows face north or south when chewing
their cud, conforming to the earth's magnetic pull,
or flower-carrying crocodiles

give their juniors piggyback rides,
or the way my thirteen-month schnoodle
chases her tail for several rounds

until she catches up, then unwinds again—
same motivation that made a Neanderthal,
weary from hunting or gathering berries,

stencil dozens of hands on a cave wall
in Maltravieso, like the palm prints
we call art on school bulletin boards—

same reason *Homo sapiens* picked up
a bird bone 42,000 years ago and gouged
holes to shape the sound of breath rushing

through its length—the first flute—left
for us to find in Geissenkloesterle cave,
or a Bronze Age elder put stylus to tablets of clay

to wedge-shape the first cuneiform words?
If it's true that all behavior of living things
advances the survival dial a notch,

then you'd probably stick to theories
of adaptive jumps for seizing airborne prey,
or enacting a fail-safe courtship display,

or gulping in air to maintain even-keeled buoyancy,
and you might not even recognize joy as it flies
up and splashes you in the face.

III

BY ANY OTHER NAME

Spanish approximates my "rose" with "rosa"
and likewise in Portuguese, but she blooms

to "roos" in Dutch, "ruusu" in Finish,
and in Hindi to "gulaab ka phool."

"Rozi" in Amharic, "woz" in Creole,
the French ones ripen to « rose » itself,

lazing in guillemets: sideways
double chevrons favored by Josephine—

guillemets derived from « Guillaume »
meaning « William », just as the Irish

strew Erse with « Liamóg » from « Liam ».
Like geese, they work in pairs,

borrowing what's said by someone else,
faithful, for all we know, to dying words:

Dickinson's "I must go in, the fog is rising."
Duncan's "Adieu, mes amis. Je vais à la gloire."

They adorn translations, like the jewels
Napoleon looted from Luxor.

Mismatched—one open, one closed—
yet they make no sense without the other,

like long-married couples—of one mind
for what gets walled out or in:

"We love the things we love for what they are."
Don't rend them asunder

through malice, mistake or sleight of hand:
they shall be unbound—"nevermore!"

ODE TO THREE EXES

Ex-husbands, like other catastrophes, come in threes.
One dead, one fled to New York, and one out of touch.
The lost-and-found blues can be sung in any key.

Sometimes the one who's left is the one who leaves
first, after years holding close the same grudge.
Ex-husbands—leavers or left—come in threes.

If shoe hits glass or glass hits shoe to seal
the chuppah vows, it's always the glass that gets crushed.
The lost-and-found blues can be sung. In any key,

"Erev Shel Shoshanim" will not guarantee
eternal evenings of roses and coos of doves.
Ex-husbands, like celebrity deaths, come in threes—

even marriages outside the fold. Years
later, a new wedding band, and with luck
the lost-and-found blues won't be sung in my key

and no one will add to the wake of decrees,
voided ketubahs and deeds covered in dust.
The lost-and-found blues can be sung in a brighter key.
Ex-husbands (count them!) come in threes.

STILL-LIFE IN ORANGE

Your poplar, in leafy underthings, barely
shows signs of the turning season,
not counting the color daubed on its crown
absorbing the sun at midday and all the hues

of the spectrum except for the one it rejects—
the color of realgar, the ruby of arsenic,
that pigment the Egyptians brushed
onto faces carved into walls of tombs;

the color of robes worn by Buddhist monks
wandering the earth with their begging bowls,
dye made from heartwood of jackfruit trees;
stockings and sleeves of a Renoir clown;

a van Gogh *Venus* with humpback moon;
Monet's haystacks, Lord Leighton's *Flaming June*,
Toulouse-Lautrec's Jane Avril in cancan petticoats—
forces of its undoing already set in motion

and the tree, after so many cycles of leaves
and no-leaves no longer dreads the endgame
and lets the leave-taking happen again,
knowing dead isn't necessarily dead, except

for when it is, like trees left standing
despite being hollowed from inside out

by beetles or drought or just bad luck—like your nearby
oak—the one riffing yellow-red each fall

until one year it didn't, and though you waited
for spring before craning your neck to check
if buds would dot the uppermost branches,
like *Pollard Willows at Setting Sun*, it stood bare.

ANT HILLS

Build your house on an ant hill
if you're tired of living alone.
Even if windows are sealed
and a blanket wedged in the space
beneath your bedroom door,
they will find a way in.
Let them come.
They can help you get past a season
of cold, or show you how purpose
gives form to the day.
They can teach you the language of trees.
Bred to bear twenty to fifty times
their collective body weight,
they can carry away your fears,
one by one, to the deepest reach
or bring you small crystals of garnets
unearthed from below—fire-eyed.

IN DEFENSE OF POLYAMORY

Because:

I can flit from mouth to open mouth, margaritas making me
bold.

there's safety in numbers, no one heart exposed,
    all licking the same honeyed rim.

lies spread like oil, indelibly stain.

I can cite the pitfalls of married love: assembly-line moves break-
    down over time.

things transformed revert to what they are.

my uncle's earnings were drawn and quartered by four ex-wives.

gifts of the flesh come in pairs to be parted and shared.

clematis, flax and eglantine, handfasted, endure.

fire—*that one in a lifetime*—never stops burning.

if you say goodbye to a moon on Jones Beach, it won't wait
    for you on the other side of the world.

BOOKENDS

Rosh Hashanah and Yom Kippur: bookends
for the ten days I join the aisle of believers,
making amends for the past year's sins—
each one counted, fist to chest—though flawed
as I am with having been stiff-necked,
succumbing to grudges, weakness of will,
I know I will never be able to remember—
should I live as long as Sarah—
all the transgressions,
planted within my body,

dormant as cancer cells that hopped a ride
on a vessel of blood, maybe years ago,
even before you felt the main tumor
growing, like greed, close to the heart.
Day Five's sundown: the precise midpoint
for these days of atonement, days of awe,
knowing nothing lasts long in the middle—
a space that can't be contained as it morphs
from what was to what will be.
The too-cold porridge, once too hot,

may soon end up spooned down the drain.
Mid-phase, mid-phrase, *in media res*
dazzle with their chimeric truths.
A midsummer's eve gradually concedes

to the equinox, the growing chill.
There and here: bookends, say, for a season
of blessings, but sometimes hard
to know if you're halfway between
the beginning and end until you're there,
just as no one living right after the fall

of Rome could define that time
as the Middle Ages—dark, perhaps,
but you need to know light to know dark.
Before the first night star appears
and the gates close as the Neilah service ends,
when the staccato teruah of the ram's horn sounds—
after the moan of the tekiah, I pray
for loved ones hovering above,
and pray to be sealed in the Book of Life—
the tekiah gedolah held as breath allows.

ETIOLOGY

Don't tell me my night owl ways
or my penchant for push-up plunge
or my sugary cravings
are to blame for the cancer
that overran the ducts
in my too-willing flesh—
things I did to myself,
like taking pregnenolone
well past the age I should have paused,
or aborting a fetus with cyst-riddled
kidneys at twenty-three weeks.

Don't blame it on misguided love.

Make me believe the fault lies
in something inhaled, ingested,
absorbed through open pores,
or in suspect genes snaking
unseen through the family tree,
like that birth defect my parents
each blamed the other for,
with one in four odds my babies
would carry the fatal code
and not survive past one day.

Better yet, convince me
an excess of black bile

from the spleen is the cause,
concentrating in the breast
just above my heart, hell-bent
on breaching the sentinel node
and merging with blood
for distant, dormant ports—
so sanguine, yet pregnable
through arsenic poultice, a purge.

TRISOMY

Confused contusions up and down my spine,
and I wouldn't mind another shot
of some kind to numb past numbness

my mute hands, my mutinous thighs
that cannot hold this separate life inside,
who only knows the roar of my bleating heart,

my blood-lit walls. Pinball life, blind
to this world, blind to the next,
you ricochet past the needle's reach,

retreat with your white flag raised—
white as the sterile pad on which I lie,
white as this hospital gown.

You cower close to my ribs, your only kin.
You can't outrun the drugs that stop your lungs
nor the standby scalpel's blade.

Don't try to lunge from what comes in waves,
overcomes your only bed.
Come. Come out to the scapula's play.

DOG STAR

for Gigi, on the first anniversary of her dying

For loyalty's sake let's grant her kind
their due, as even in biblical Egypt
no dogs barked when the Israelites fled.
Talmudic scholars might lend her
the animal soul—the *nefesh*—let it reside
in her blood, though they'd deny her
that divine spark—the *neshama*—
that would allow her to ponder the difference.

Did you know that the ancient Egyptians
convinced themselves that the heart
housed the so-called human soul,
and death sealed one's fate by weight—
heart versus feather—the lighter the better—
though pharaohs got a free pass to ascend?

Do the best dogs get to become one
with Sirius—the size of two suns
and twenty-five times more luminous,
whose dogged fetch and return
ancient astronomers tracked per annum
each time the Nile overran its banks?

And now in these Days of Awe of early fall,
Sirius sits low in the nighttime sky.
We Jews scour our sins, like stains,
and remember our dead—human or beast.

After the shofar sounds one last time,
the Book of Life will be sealed for the year,
and we'll look to the sky for that first star
to signal the end of Yom Kippur's fast,
when the first bite of food to breach our lips
tastes sweetest after a day of going without,
and a star might wag its diaphanous tail
even in the darkest of nights.
What after all is a soul?

If you mess with the Good Book,
you might mistake the Hebrew "ray" for "horn"—
karan and *keren* easy to confuse—and like Michelangelo,
envision Moses at Sinai with horns on his head
instead of suffused with a heavenly glow—

another gift from the God of Stone Tablets.
So much depends on a single vowel issuing forth
from the rattling depths of a throat, as in last words,
when meaning shapes lips gasping for breath—
perhaps one small clue about the afterlife—

or your son's ex-girlfriend who conversed
with God despite the haze of Haldol dispensed each day
in pulp-free orange juice—new translations
thanks to missed doses—squeezing
that divine voice from the pulpit of her dreaming.

In another time you might have paid a price
for putting the Word in other words,
like William Tyndale, strangled then set on fire
or John Wycliffe, ashes strewn along the River Swift
for wrestling with the sacred in your native tongue.

WE WEREN'T SO JEWISH THEN

Dangling our faith on a golden chain,
we gave our children Old Testament
names like Matthew and Aaron and Ruth
to honor the family dead
piling up faster by the year—

a whirlwind of covered mirrors, black
ribbons, and yahrzeit candles burning
in glass—and words like *brucha* and *yizkor*
at graveside prayer, layering stone
upon stone like ancient tropes,

but still we wedded outside the tribe,
drawn to men who'd never donned a skullcap,
yet stomped on glass, timid shards
in their soles, to prove their accepting love—
our mothers, defied, turned away and closed

their eyes each Shabbat, gathering
candlelight in their hands—a vigil
to combat the dark they feared
we'd brought upon ourselves—more dreadful
than any epithet sprayed on our walls.

ODALISQUE

Nude, like a Matisse, lounged
under the hard eyes of years,
semi-reclined in a slat-backed chair
draped in green passing for silk

her then husband-artist could ill afford.
In the upper left, a '70s Brookland view with slow-
to-gentrify homes robed themselves in muted citrus.
A patch of sky mottled baby-blue: a sign

her second child would die the day he was born.
Her eyes look down, allowing us
to consider at leisure her curves, the creamy
expanse on her left, relieved

by the areola's blush, nipple not yet nursed
by a child, nor pierced by a sentinel node probe
or what cannot be foretold: cells gone deeply
wild in the ducts of her breast,

their tell-tale sonic tracks only exposed
to a trained naked eye;
scalpel's thrusts goading the too-close heart,
then once again, doubling the old suture line,

leaving a scar nearly unseen, but for that extra pucker
of skin, as if taking in a blouse.

And taking us in she lets us know she knows
she will always look the same.

SEQUOIA

Immune to lightning and Arctic cold,
floods and burning blasts of wind
down Sierra Nevada slopes—
everything nature can dish out—
it was made to last three thousand years
and could have grown to three hundred feet,
could have survived another half-millennium—
Earth's largest on Earth, though saddled
like the rest of us, with time—
could have succumbed to a natural end,
brought down by its own heft
to the forest floor, a regal
final resting place, there among
the yellow pines, white firs,
there where it had stood before native tribes
surrendered its shade, before whale oil
was rendered to light—but now,
weakened by drought stress and fire,
invaded by beetles carving elegant runes
in its bark, it has died, like Benkei,
a giant warrior monk, standing upright.

My mother was not afraid of the dark,
or the abstracts she outlined in black
of her last years—black as the feathers
of the raven tasked with finding signs
of land—maybe a leaf from an olive tree—
but never returned to the ark,
distracted by hunger for water-logged corpses
left in the great flood's wake.

Hers was the first light I knew,
diffused through the swoosh of blood
she played by heart, like the Chopin
nocturnes she'd coax from piano keys
even after I'd been released
from the holding room she'd built
from her own timbered flesh.

Chopin starved and struggled for music's
sake, preferring to play piano in the dark.
Almost half of his "songs of the night"
were composed in minor keys,
and all with broken chords supporting
mysterious melodies floating like doves,
like his own heart, now preserved in a jar

of cognac, buried in a pillar
of an old Warsaw church.
                              "Mother,
my poor mother," were his last words.

Mine was the last voice my mother sensed
in the shadowy space between breaths,
eyelids no longer fluttering between worlds,
mouth too slack to form words from the air.
Only the pulse in her neck kept time,
obeying the metronome meter implanted
in her chest.
              I like to think that even beyond
her heart's last beat she could still hear
my nightingale song, cheering her solitude.

We practice dying a little each time,

like the German Shepherd I trained to play

dead, until the day he got carried away.

After downward-facing dogs and plows,

we release the white bird of breath

from its cage. The mind scatters.

We are lizard, cobra, dragonfly,

falling. Imperfect, we crave hyacinths.

We crave Siamese cats and vermouth.

We crave desire. We must learn

to let the body fend for itself in silence.

The heart, slack with indifference, slows.

No birds of paradise flock to our body's

leavings. We are the eye of the needle,

carrion flower, half moon, rising.

VARIATIONS ON A SAMUEL BECKETT RIFF

Every loss recalls another loss
eroding more of you, a brine-lashed cave.
The end is in the beginning yet we go on.

Grief springs out of sofas, credenzas, and drawers.
Masking and distance can't stop the ache.
Every loss recalls another loss,

like delving inside a wooden nesting doll—
the hard-to-open smallest reveals hollowed space.
The end is in the beginning. We go on

despite the empty chairs and beds—the way they'd want
us to, to hell with booby-trapped DNA.
Every loss recalls another loss.

Cut out the troubled cells—offer a leg or an arm
or even two—you'll still feel the phantom pain.
The end is in the beginning. Going on,

we learn to patiently sift through day-to-day dross
for the words to divine the endgame.
Every loss recalls another loss.
The end is in the beginning. Go on.

FINDING / KEEPING THE BEAT

My fingers were taught to translate / hold
and release each scored note

measured / poured bar to bar
on a musical staff, varying touch

on a piano's keys or pulling / bowing
rosined horsehair against

catgut strings, left ear lowered,
straining toward a well-tempered bridge.

My near-perfect pitch could muster
an orchestra "A" / a doorbell's chime

in the absence / shadow of sound,
confirming Mozart's belief that music lies

in the silence between notes,
not unlike the open spaces I'd later learn

to range by stroking / wheedling keyboards
synched to computer displays,

and though my voice was limited
by words that wouldn't stick in my head,

here I could improvise,
count / compose stresses stretched over lines

dangling with dissonance, restless / flirting
cursor hungry to reach the tonic chord.

Acknowledgments

I wish to extend my heartfelt gratitude to the editors of the following literary journals where these poems first appeared, some in earlier versions:

The Arlington Literary Journal (ArLiJo): "After I Swallowed the Willow Tree;" "Corpse Pose"

The Bellingham Review: "Out of an Absence of Caution;" "Small Griefs"

Beltway Poetry Quarterly: "After I Xeroxed the Sky;" "Lockdown Aubade on Rimsky-Korsakov's Birthday;" "Zooming to Elysian Fields"

Blue Lyra Review: "Ant Hills"

Bourgeon: "Good Sense;" "Ode for Three Exes"

Colorado Review: "In Other Words;" "Of the Fourth Platonic Virtue"

Denver Quarterly: "After I Swallowed the Willow Tree;" "Painted Moon;" "Tintoretto Blues;" "Trisomy"

Écrire aux Amériques: "Quarantine: Day 40"

Five Points: "Odalisque;" "Vigilance"

Gargoyle: "An Excess of Dreaming;" "By Any Other Name;" "Calder's Menagerie"

Interim: "In Defense of Polyamory"

The Journal of the American Medical Association (JAMA): "Sequelae;" "Viva the Vagus"

Los Angeles Review: "Translating the Dead"

Medmic: "Aubade;" "Everything in nature contains its violence"

North American Review: "My Goyishe Ex-Husband"

Notre Dame Review: "Coming To;" "Forever-Bound"

On the Seawall: "Translating the Body;" "Why Sturgeon Leap"

Passager: "Variations on a Samuel Beckett Riff"

Phoebe: "After I Xeroxed the Sky" (Finalist and Honorable Mention, Greg Grummer Prize, judged by Bin Ramke)

Plume: "Sequoia"

Poetica: "Bookends;" "Feast of Tabernacles"

Potomac Review: "Dog Star;" "We Weren't So Jewish Then"

Spoon River Poetry Review: "Decreation;" "Finding/Keeping the Beat"

Vingt ans après le 9/11: "Lockdown Aubade on Rimsky-Korsakov's Birthday"

~

This collection could not have been completed without the encouragement and love of my husband, Ted Miller, who patiently served as a sounding board for my word choice struggles on a daily basis. I am also deeply indebted to Jeffrey Levine, who has accompanied me on this book's journey from the start. Thanks are also due to Roger Greenwald, my trusted grammarian and friend, the late Stanley Plumly, for his wisdom, and to the following friends who were also my first readers, including Tina Daub, Brandel France de Bravo, Lola Haskins, Carol Quinn, Katherine Smith, Jeneva Stone, and Martha Young. Finally, my deep appreciation goes to my Seagull family, including Naveen Kishore, whose support of my work has never wavered; Sunandini Banerjee, for her stunning cover designs; Sayoni Ghosh, for her spot-on edits and suggestions; and Bishan Samaddar, for his literary expertise and for always being there for me.